one of our skylarks

ALISON BIELSKI

Published by Cinnamon Press
Meirion House, Glan yr afon, Tanygrisiau
Blaenau Ffestiniog, Gwynedd, LL41 3SU
www.cinnamonpress.com

ISBN: 978-1-907090-21-9
British Library Cataloguing in Publication Data. A CIP record for
this book can be obtained from the British Library.

Designed and ty~~~~ over
design by Cottia F~

Printed in Poland

Cinnamon Press Ltd
www.inpressbook ooks
Council www.cllc.

The publisher acknowledges the financial assistance of the Welsh
Books Council

Acknowledgements

Thanks are due to the editors of publications in which some of the
poems first appeared and to organisations that have supported
the writing: *Acumen; Coastline* (Dewi Roberts); Gwent Poetry
Society, *The Interpreter's House, New Welsh Review; Pembroke
Magazine,* USA; *Quattrocento; Roundyhouse*; Society of Women
Writers and Journalists; *The Third Day* (Gomer) and The
University of Wales, Aberystwyth.

Contents

travelling north:

for Sally

"Skylark —its voice is unmistakeable"
         —*Charles Swainson, 1886*

one of our skylarks

around the south

5 ways to cross River Severn

stand beside pebbled Broad Stone
hoping to be rowed across

watch Beachley ferry approach
your car will glide on water

rattle through black train tunnel
water roars above your head

leave Severn suspension bridge
now Second Crossing curves green

fly east from Cardiff airport
hover over grey tide-race

in limbo between countries
now you belong to neither

tidal footprints

tracks on Severn shore
    make Stone Age trails
two men leading one child
    to fishing grounds

Uskmouth still remains
    quite unaware
foraging humans left
    live history

Queen Stone

Forest of Dean

I cannot sit here
alone on the Queen Stone
it unnerves me with
traditions of cruelty
and sacrifice reminding
me of love's brevity

so climb up beside me
over druid grooves
which raised their varnished platform
watch from the summit
as this unchanged Wye valley
unrolls summer colour

when our hands press warmly
gritstone shrinks to its
cold core and all that
matters is our own closeness
high up on the Queen Stone
caught in Wye's fleeting summer

wreck of a Bristol trader

I Herbert Stevens of Whitson
will tell you of disaster
these Levels can never forget

in that storm a Bristol trader
smashed on Severn's Channel shore
opposite Gwent's Nash lighthouse

I quickly collected neighbours
we rushed towards our landmark
struggled through mud as tide ebbed

one drowned sailor lay sprawled
on a newly exposed mudbank
four others roped to ship's mast
were also dead
                we stumbled back
carried them into Nash Church
for rest on the bellringers' floor

above us four boars' heads
stared from the tower parapet
that spire accused an absent God

Cornelius Cox of Church Farm
was expected to ring the bell
for evensong
                stood surrounded
by five corpses each movement
challenging death's stillness
every tone a passing bell

he took his place for service
bellringer among the living
followed ritual aware of
horror locked in that room
stunned we faced our future
knew tragedy blurred to history

buried city

Old Trellech, Monmouthshire

tunnels run beside city walls
moles have monopolised streets
past underground Wyeside ruins

snuffling around iron forges
they snag black fur on weapons
scenting destruction and dust
investigating middens
they glory in ordure and bones
littering fallen church steeples

greedily gorging every hour
their half-blind eyes are searching
for banquets of slithering worms

they avoid dangerous places
breed to raise naked babies
clustered in cramping hollows
unaware that overhead
one observer is finding shards
of fourteenth century treasures

soon yellow machines will clatter
across this field with armies
of enthusiasts bearing tools

then moles attempting to surface
will alert watching kestrels
but some escaping talons
may reach their Summer Country
where in subterranean peace
they will dig their own new city

crossover

Caerleon, Gwent

something is wrong
with this bridge
spanning River Usk

its foundation stone
added to late repairs
is carved with
wrong date
wrong designer
wrong builder
ON THE WRONG BRIDGE

We are all deceived
no credit now given
to local men
their identity
stolen away
by NEWPORT

that stone appeared
outside our own
Legionary Museum
considered local
was inserted
as proud landmark

drive over this bridge
but do not believe
what you have read
only stone curves
and Usk River are real

delayed return

Mrs. Williams, wife of Edward Williams, brazier of Caerleon, Gwent.
29th October 1772

almost home. she stepped on wooden bridge
balanced her lantern above Usk tide
heard that tearing sound
                              flung against
torn railings was suddenly hurtled
down river on one piece of ragged
platform wide as her cottage room

she cried out but neighbours approaching
helplessly stared unable to reach
her raft bound for St. Julian's
she screamed at dimly lighted houses
no answer met her lonely distress
as waves raced nearer Newport bridge

one pier halted splintering planking
left waters rushing to open sea
save me save me she yelled into
midnight blackness still clinging to rails
pregnant so swaying above timber
then one light glittered through blown spray

from a moored barge
                              its master alert
heard calls penetrate thunder torrent
launched his boat struggled out blindly
until clear moon surprised and he found
this desperate woman, threw out rope
attempted to calm her terror

he rowed her from bridge to shore shelter
where they waited for dawn's arrival
he took her to Newport to rest
but she woke anxious for family
soon homebound in a cart sat wrapped as
the horse trotted through eastern Gwent

she had no need to grip wooden rails
and floorboards were nailed down securely
they passed fields and deep-rooted trees
where she caught silver glimpses of Usk
slithering on its treacherous way
between rough banks of undergrowth

her cocooned child slept in darkness
awaiting its own time to be born
from waters into dry morning light

Gwent tragedy

nobody saw their car crash
on this unlit coastal road
Caldicot's hidden ditches
covered four fatal drownings
daylight revealing terror

tragedy on bleak wetlands
where four centuries ago
one tumbling Severn floodtide
wrecked twenty-six parishes

deep reens bordered with willow
and upright yellow iris
fringe Levels' treacherous edge
today only jagged grass
marks horror of young men's loss

bridge builder

David Evans, Architect

every day he sees Pontypridd's bridge
built by his father to span the Taff
its curve encircles his childhood
he cleans tools running errands
watches William choosing stones
one day he thinks *I shall create*
another larger Bridge of Beauty
to conquer Newport's giant tides
I shall bridge the River Usk

so he learns slowly through long
apprenticeship years struggles
at night with mathematics
drawing plans working out stresses
until poised on Newport's timber
walkway shuddering over Usk
he decides *this stone bridge needs*
five arches with central span
of seventy feet sprung from piers

money is raised by share flotation
still he fights battles in his mind
with forty-foot tides slamming stone
complete as the century turns
David Evans surveys his work
this river runs through his blood
carrying forbears towards Severn
he has tamed dangerous Usk
linking shores with vision in stone

breaking silence

Sugar Loaf Mountain, Abergavenny

mae wedi myned yn abred gwyllt
— *Welsh proverb*

severed by slashing blades
brambles die hacked to ground
scout spades uncover walls

this mountain village startles
abandoned to decay
by overtaxed families

we do not know their names
but teams clearing brambles
revive speech and laughter

this mountain is alive

visit to a grave

St. Woolos Cemetery, Newport

marigolds blaze on your grave
in our seven-hilled hometown
deprived of earth stems protest
tracing shapes across your name
painting shadows on granite

closing pedestrian gates
I turn to observe orange
obscuring that final date
sun strikes one frozen angel
warms her with summer colour

green gift

Belle Vue Park, Newport

Belle Vue
across docks' blackened tide
but here green envelops
promenade terrace reflects
pagoda bandstand roof
while Lord Tredegar's landgift
pleases weekend strollers

Belle Vue
over glasshouses past
bowling green tennis courts
where skipping with two sisters
I climbed on twisted swings
seesaws and glittering slide
high above Cardiff road

wide view
neatly dressed we shuffled
carefully swept gravel
defied elusive keepers
butterflies tantalised
as we jumped to imprison
fragile vibrating wings

long view
of childhood excitement
in fluttering pleasures
those daring summer swingflights
in light skirts then scrambling
through spider-webbed shrubbery
spying on bowlers' games

Belle Vue
such vibrant energies
colour--clustered in rows
with guardian butterflies
clasping emblazoned gates
opened above the threshold
of Newport's Otherworld

stonefern

Cwmtillery Colliery

released from that rattling cage
we file between tramrails
stumbling to unseen coalface
soon this mine will be closed
its pumps finally silenced
these workings under flood

we pass between scraped walls
trellised with forest fernprints
suddenly coal gleams black
so we crawl in dusty jeans
through half a metre's height
each pick one loosened nugget

props arch over hard hats
hold back that ceiling of rock
warning us to escape
from this tunnelled underworld
we read earth's history
in fossil tendrils of fern

no hands

Crickhowell

I heard you read our poem
last night. today I left
stopping off at Crickhowell
missing your loving touch

I walked into the church
where nobody greeted me
longing for you clawed my skin

I saw that effigy
of Lady Sybil Paunceforte
who sent both cut-off hands
to ransom her snatched husband

blank streets led me away
sunlight struck with its knifeblade

Swan River

Rumney, Cardiff

hypermarkets float
on rafted marshland
bordering Newport Road
Swan River survives
wide Cardiff carparks

modern swans provide
plastic shapes to sail
on a take-away pond
you can make this new
Elarch River in your
Rumney garden claim
to preserve an old
wetland tradition

without arching wings
without water-weed
the only fisherman
beside Swan River
your secretive cat

harpfields

Rhiwbina, Cardiff

I am walking on harpfields
which are modern tarmac roads
nine acres in telyn shape
I want to hear faint music
seeping from ox-ploughed furrows
I need to capture worksongs
stifling underneath townscape

back home in this top-floor flat
holding my knee harp to pluck
its colourful nylon strings
I observe Caedelyn Park
shrunk down to a curving frame
now I reinvent singing
for all these built-over fields

winter flight

one grey skein crosses sky
streaking towards Cardiff Bay
geese are migrating to Spain
that V-formation an act
of precision with wide views
their strongest bird is leader
while weaker keep in line
spaced at equal distance

      I marvel at such control
      as geese pass cedar branches
      tumbling in random gusts
      curled leaves swirl over grass
      yet that high geometry
      has evolved through centuries
      fashioned each eye each feather
      geared to flight survival

geese will return in spring
along this exact route
how many young survive
such journeys we cannot know
but watching we assemble
torn scraps of littered living
heartbreak stress brief ecstasy
clutched under seasonal skies

no substitute

twelve neon lamps flare orange
outside my Cardiff flat
I cannot find one star

only when driving at night
on roads across South Wales
does star panorama
amaze on every side

I never want such journeys
to end when I must fit
my key in that slim lock

then closing opaque night blinds
I shall cancel out glare
think of galaxies deep
in unlimited space

while trapped human travellers
glide over black tarmac
under cascades of light

progress report

cutting lake water of Cardiff Bay
the waterbus glides on with Captain
Manannan steering straight ahead
he imagines a yellow plain
rides on over covered mudflats
drowned by this modern barrage
but believes an oakwood springs
above seabed thrusting out
ripe acorns and leaves of gold

in his trance he scans distance
sees Bran rowing towards him
now waits to hail him pointing out
that landfall where red flowers
burst out beside honey rivers
his Otherworld island of Mag Mell
reality shows him Roath Basin
Mermaid Quay without mermaids
gulls strutting on Admiral's Walk

he ferries two Irish passengers
monocled poet and dramatist
who sit stiffly on cushions
Yeats and Augusta climb ashore
walk towards St. David's Hotel
where penthouse suites await them
they carry parcels of scripts
soon to be staged in Wexford
here they cannot see any swans

Manannan heads for the bar
his country has changed. scooters
flash past instead of horses
those happy women cluster round
but who can spot the Sun King
in this rainy City of Cardiff?
upstairs two dream of Abbey plays
while waterbus tugs at mooring ropes
lights on water reflect new myths

Caerphilly update

this green lady is unemployed
no longer stalking her victims
they are all at the Job Centre
or travelling down to Cardiff

this green lady in stretch mini
drifts into noisy lunchtime bars
later abandons her pick-up
after stealing his credit cards

now it is time to cling to walls
disguised as evergreen ivy
tomorrow she will shake brimstone
butterflies out of twisted hair

windsurfers at Cold Knap, Barry

between rollers it skims
across swelling Severn
birdflight with sun plumage
silhouettes balancing
on precarious boards

I stand on banked pebbles
hill high above shingle
sea limestone sky merge in
greyness only broken
by red yellow white wings

camper vans cluster round
their occupants unload
rucksacks frames rattling sails
they climb into wetsuits
black armoured against waves
carry sections to tide

leave me an onlooker
weather wrapped in fleeces
I follow launches as
owners make Icarus
fall rise anticipate
that ecstasy of speed

reclamation

Merthyr Mawr Levels

once we blamed drunken lords
or negligent well guardians
for coastline inundations

    today we are realistic
    planting trees among sand dunes
    this rippled ground still slides
    slowly to tidal Severn

        we always live with danger
        on our triple-sided coastline
        fighting this creeping threat

            now sapling roots with blackthorn
            must slow this hidden menace
            each springtime working here
            our footsteps move a little more

        inland

strange burial

Mumbles Head

carry him gently up rockpath
lay him in my cold cave

I expected cowled strangers
to arrive at sunset

exchanging agreed signs
without dangerous words

       lay him under my cell
       ivorypale in deathsleep

       I do not need gold coins
       to say mass for his soul

       oarblades mutter his name
       syllables drowning in ebbtide

markers

memorial to Petty Officer Edgar Evans, Rhossili Church, Gower

Evans your story stares from this
relief wall plaque

you froze to death
on that Antarctic expedition
with Captain Scott yet today we glimpse
one local youth leaping on shoreline
imagining lands over horizon

this church replaces an earlier
building engulfed by sand its masons'
triumph destroyed by erosion
you tumbled into disaster but numb
fingers struggle to touch the chancel
where vision died left only stone

time-lapse at Amroth

Nelson and Emma
in Amroth castle
stare out across
grass green foreshore

where roundabouts
clatter and whirl
their painted horses
leaping to music

                fairground is drowning
                one fading roundabout
                spins over breakers
                those wooden steeds

                seahorses leading
                Manannan's chariot
                over his undersea
                oakwood realm

sudden reality
shows low tide
exposing stumps
of petrified trees

no naval hero
no festival
just smothering sand
creeping to coast

beach find

near Kidwelly. Carmarthenshire

now tread carefully
you walk over bones
sea drowned this village
crushed me buried me
deep under pebbles

tide moulded sand dunes
with sliding fingers
no trace of my home
remains but if you

find one broken coin
think of this fisher
living on threshold
between two worlds where
rules are meaningless

keep that single piece
polish it to bronze
my memorial
snatched from destruction

postcard from Tenby

suddenly on this bleak october day
blue jewel sea flashes on shadowed floor
our postman sheds his catalogue cascade
but one rare treasure tumbles from my door
our circle turns reversing in slow time
I once mailed greetings from my coastal home
now round these inland flats land is defined
by shelter belts and grass carefully mown
when apple trees explode in foaming showers
I see white rollers racing up South Beach
at night I miss each rocking tide's slow power
as gulls give way to barn owl's hunting screech
now on my desk rekindled summer glows
cancelling distance with three words of prose

not Grantchester

Marbell Chapel, Llanybri

this clock carved in stone
sited on Marbell tower
defies time with hands
at five to ten forever

eighteen seventy nine
offers no explanation
marks an event forgotten
fire plague or celebration

such time is static holds
no hope of honeyed tea
we leave here still confused
hours move on silently

the truth of trees

Nevern Churchyard

yew trees lining ancient ways
bleed continual resin
rising up from killers' graves

yews live for one thousand years
oozing their crimson lifeblood
human wars outlast all trees

travelling north

breaking surface

Llangorse lake

jetskis are silenced
night creeps across water
pallid moondisc stares
over lake's late smoothness

our human breathing
    slow-tuned to thin ripples
        finds urgent rhythms
           whispering sunken tales
          of that kingly court
        its orchards neat gardens
      raised on this crannog
built in our sacred lake

such brief night respite
now offers us legends
before day's tourists
cut surface with new toys

yellow surprise

Brecon Beacons

unremarked yet unique
this name Silurian Hawkweed
proves my alpine ancestry
     I survived creeping Ice Age
     my seed dormant beneath
     frozen killer layers until
     thaw secured my release

rescued from oblivion
I unfurled radial petals
to mimic flaming sun
poised above Welsh mountains

I thrive bathed in moisture
from waterfall's cool shower
hurtling through splintered rock
     my upright stems store power
     I celebrate survival
     explode with yellow energy
     dazzle this tarmac road

visit from Mr. Shelley

Cwmelan, Elan Valley

there he was at my door
wearing a cap with his
neck bare and holding
the gift in long fingers

for me Elizabeth Jones
who had carried his post
and seen on hall table
that small brass kettle

he would not stay but
placed it on my cupboard
so I polished metal
as bright as sunlight

then filled and set it
on the trivet to boil
over slow peat fire
soon water heating

sent up bubbles
I heard them whisper
flooding this valley
I shall cover his house

overwhelm his garden
one day he will drown
I listened appalled and saw
Mr. Shelley had closed the gate

blue paperweight

Welsh Royal Crystal, Rhayader

you contain fire and earth
came glowing from furnace
on a long metal rod
to be shaped then cooled
smoothed under water flow
by craftsmen who travelled
each day from Cardiff

you are stained sea-blue
have left elements
and cutting wheel behind
now dry and so cold
you balance on my palm
a glass skydome already
capturing sunlife

if I leave you fire
will smoulder as rays
concentrate in your heart
so I place you on papers
to guard my written poem
you write its final draft
in blue refracted light

red kites

Gigrin Farm, Rhayader

through mist glitter we watch kites
cutting cloud with scissor tails

however high we climb they defy us
circling out of human reach

diving and swerving in currents
while we rest in clumsy clothes

envying their survival kit
of basic claw and eye

they are breeding again in Wales
we count from hillside farm

always below always earthbound
staring upwards into sky

water-break-its-neck

Radnor Forest

water tumbles over rock
where every ledge sprouts living green
standing in this running stream
we breathe new freshness as we look

through dripping trees towards that rlm
where hurtling into sudden space
energy and power replace
each unimportant human aim

the reason for yarrow

New Radnor

springing from castle yard
white-petalled yarrow heads
unfold nourished on blood
from that murdered garrison

this staunching plant with use
first taught to Achilles
spread across battle sites
through centuries of slaughter

white roots invade this site
of violence while deep
serrated leaves contrast
with circular flowerheads

bearing centred yellow
suns preparing to seed
across those buried stones
into our warring future

ordeal

Idris sits on his platform chair
he is not mad but a poet
marooned as high as Cadair
he rustles papers stares out
towards that waiting audience
red kites are soaring above him
or is it a that faulty light bulb?

soon he will have to perform
quickly gaining attention
those upturned faces unnerve him
he transforms them into scattered
pebbles clinging to mountain ridge
finds one sudden alpine flower
rare plant smiling encouragement

now he is poised on cold summit
papers flutter up into clouds
his voice tumbles over slopes
a blustering wind gust brings
outburst of clapping—his ordeal
becomes a triumph—he is mad
who else would choose the giant's chair?

illusion

a Llanberis loss

when you stepped from this lake
dripping yet radiant
I offered you an apple

my sudden longing blossomed
as we moved along shoreline
strolling slowly together

> our two worlds began merging
> but you kept strange secrets
> while I possessed no guile

> yet we heard subtle music
> from one silver apple branch
> shaken in Otherworld mist

I know loving is fleeting
when young I still believed
passion would never fade

yet you fled after blows
diving into lake depths
shattered my trust in dreaming

slate poem with one touch of red

he plunges into Nantlle's quarry
water cancels out reflections

divers race to hills of slate
wetsuits crowd this fenced-off rim

an Irish hero swam black tarn
defied taboo of death by water

Fraoch plucked berries as requested
from island rowan's laden branch

now boys awaiting surface ripples
see dappled red of long lost fruit

where slender trees fell into mines
as Romans tunnelled under rockface

silence
          stillness
                    sudden horror
drowned he sinks in jagged depths

again one youthful sacrifice
snatched in revenge for desecration

rain turns all to monochrome
police arrive
                boys stand appalled

climbing challenge

Dinorwic Slate Quarry, North Wales

such narrow handholds hide
edges in smooth slate wall
thin fingers probe each flaw
breaking this vertical

to balance angled limbs
each gripping hand competes
controlling body strain
from head to unseen feet

slowly you climb upwards
with body parallel
to sun reflecting slate
halfway towards your goal

braced for that final thrust
over wide broken lip
your eyes adjust to glare
dazzling across summit

you wave to us below
now you can stand erect
brief visitor to this
once dynamited ledge

roped for weekend practice
you scaled this height alone
proving new leisure skills
can conquer mountain stone

diversity

Snowdonia

three survivors
of arctic ice
sorrel stonecrop
rare saxifrage

we flower safe
from hungry sheep
hidden by this
crevice lip

purple then yellow
petals rise
from varied branches
cramped for space

battering storms
race overhead
rooted in rock
we set our seed

one of our skylarks is missing

rising into blue ether
that questing skylark poses
unanswerable questions
to its skyborne audience
who heckle it to silence

under my landmark white rock
I David Owen trap notes
yet this hijacked melody
cannot prevent one human
act of cruelty on earth

Anglesey legend

when his harpist died
final notes scattered
 at Gruffudd's side

his shattered harp
slithered overboard
that escaping ship

       with court restored
       Gruffudd's new harpist
       plucked rising rhythms

       which guided fingers
       through surfacing chords
       suddenly new

links

St. Cwyfan's Church, Anglesey

so difficult to approach
except at low tide
you must arrive here on foot
to view my seawalls

I have something to explain
as you tread my smooth nave
where one aisle is demolished
my fight for survival
against creeping erosion

when finally I lie drowned
severed from shrunk mainland
on sunken paths smothered by
weed and clustering shells

do not expect me to be
silent for I shall still
murmur my joyful response
to your gatherings held
at the newer inland church

and when you see saved relics
think of my loneliness
shattered as I unlock doors
to welcome you give strength
to meet this new century

links 2

I cross your stone thrown beach
to celebrate survival
while congregation sings
to wave's warning cadences

       now tumbling seagulls perch
       screaming on crumbled walls

as tide destroys foundations
vibrations will remain
your final protest reaching
all passing fishing crews